IGOR STRAVINS

L'OISEAU DE
THE FIREBIRD
DER FEUERVOGEL

Ballet Suite 1945
for Orchestra

Ernst Eulenburg Ltd

London · Mainz · Madrid · New York · Paris · Prague · Tokyo · Toronto · Zürich

CONTENTS

PREFACE

Stravinsky's early works *Fireworks* and *Scherzo fantastique* were performed for the first time on 6 February 1909 in a concert in St Petersburg conducted by Alexander Siloti. In the audience was Sergey Diaghilev, who was impressed by Stravinsky's compositions and was to play a distinctive role in the further course of Stravinsky's life. As the young composer's teacher, Nikolay Rimsky-Korsakov, had died on 8 June 1908, Stravinsky was looking for a new patron who could present him to the public. Since 1906 Diaghilev had transferred his main activities to Paris, where he had organised five orchestral concerts in 1907 and a season of five ballets in 1909. To Diaghilev's circle belonged the dancer and choreographer Mikhail Fokine, the painter Leon Bakst, the dancer Vaslav Nijinsky and the prima ballerina Tamara Karsavina. According to his *Chroniques de ma vie*, Stravinsky wanted 'to join this group of progressive and energetic artists, of which Diaghilev was the soul'.

Stravinsky's first commissions were to orchestrate Chopin's Nocturne in A flat and Valse brillante in E flat for the ballet *Les Sylphides* and Grieg's *Kobold* for *Le Festin* (both in 1909), the latter being a divertissement to music by various composers. While the Russian dancers of the Ballets Russes were already celebrating triumphs in Paris, Stravinsky was finishing the first act of his opera *The Nightingale* in Ustilug.

The criticism in the French press of the lack of Russian colour or Russian atmosphere (i.e. of folk elements) in the Ballets Russes caused Diaghilev to choose material that would set the Russian aspect more firmly in the foreground. He decided on the fairy tale of the Firebird, in which elements of various other Russian tales were integrated.

The synopsis: the Tsarevich Ivan one day sees a wonderful Firebird. He pursues it but succeeds only in seizing a golden feather from it. His pursuit leads him into the realm of the evil Kashchei, an immortal demi-god, who wishes to catch him and turn him, like numerous other knights and princes, into stone. Kashchei's daughters and the 13 captive princesses intervene and endeavour to rescue Ivan. The Firebird appears and lifts the spell by revealing to Ivan the secret of Kashchei's immortality. Through the breaking of the egg which was kept in a casket, Kashchei loses his life along with his magic power. His castle vanishes, and the maidens, the princesses and Ivan seize the golden apples of his garden.

The scenario, to which Nijinsky, Bakst and Benois also contributed, emerged under Fokine's direction. He had requested a 'Russian ballet' from Anatoly Lyadov, who had originally been entrusted with its composition by Diaghilev. When it proved that Nikolay Tcherepnin's sketches for music for *The Firebird* were unsatisfactory and Lyadov would hardly be in a position to have the composition ready in the time allotted, Diaghilev decided on Stravinsky, who knew how to make use of this opportunity. In the autumn of 1909, after returning to St Petersburg, he began on the composition of *The Firebird*, although he could not yet be sure of eventually obtaining the commission to compose the ballet, for which a fee of 1000 roubles was finally agreed. Not until a month after beginning on the composition did Diaghilev come to St Petersburg in December; and he was astonished that Stravinsky had already started work on it. From the beginning of November Stravinsky had withdrawn to the Rimsky-Korsakov family's dacha to the south-east of St Petersburg: in December he returned to St Petersburg, where until March he completed the composition. Stravinsky played over the new work on the piano to Diaghilev and his circle in the house on Zamiatin Pereulok, and attended the rehearsals of the Ballets Russes after Fokine had arranged the choreography for those scenes which were already written. Stravinsky completed the instrumentation of the orchestral score a month later. The ballet company travelled to Paris in the new year. In mid-April the score was sent to Paris, where in May, during his first stay in the city, Stravinsky corrected further details and dated the score 18 May 1910. The autograph is today preserved in the Bibliotheca Bodmeriana in Cologny (Geneva) and is owned by the Geneva Conservatoire.

The opulent scenery and some of the costumes were created by Alexander Golovin, the other costumes (Firebird, Tsarevich and Tsarevna) by Leon Bakst. The work, conducted by Gabriel Pierné had its extremely successful première on 25 June 1910 at the Paris Opéra. The principal dancers were Tamara Karsavina (Firebird), Vera Fokina (Tsarevna), Mikhail Fokine (Tsarevich) and Alexis Bulgakov (Kashchei). During the performances Stravinsky for the first time made the acquaintance (in Diaghilev's box) of the Parisian celebrities Proust, Giraudoux, Claudel, St John Perse, Sarah Bernhardt and the musicians Ravel and Debussy, with whom a friendly relationship lasted until Debussy's death. In the course of the first performance, Diaghilev went so far as to allow horses to be brought on to the stage – an effect which however, was not repeated. Fokine sought balletic expressiveness in the realization of the rhythm, not in mimicry. Evil was represented by grotesque, angular, ugly and even comic gestures. The monsters bad to crawl on all fours, to jump like frogs or to make virtuosic leaps. The princesses danced barefoot, moved gracefully and smoothly, while only the Firebird was represented by a dancer on points, who had to execute many difficult leaps. According to Stravinsky's later opinion, the princesses danced with insipid sweetness, while the male dancers portrayed the extremes of rough masculinity and ferocity; in the Kashchei scene the men dancers, sitting on the ground, stupidly thrust their feet back and forth. George Balanchine's choreography from the years 1949–50 is preferable to Fokine's, according to Stravinsky; the composer also felt that the costumes created by Chagall in 1945 and retained in performances by the New York City Ballet until 1970 were, on the whole, the most successful. From the correspondence and private diaries of Gide, Claudel, Proust and others it is clear that it was particularly the discipline and virtuosity of the soloists and the emphasis on male dancers in the Ballets Russes which captivated the spectators and the intellectuals.

The decisive factor in the success of the ballet, whose action can be termed rather schematic and undramatic, was Stravinsky's music, which Anna Pavlova had rejected as too complicated and too meaningless. The music of *The Firebird* made Stravinsky famous at a stroke. Even today it is among the most popular pieces of the 20th century in general. *The Firebird* was also one of the few ballets to remain in the repertoire of the Ballets Russes. The composer himself, however, was not satisfied with the original version, which was published in 1910 by Jurgenson and later by Schott. He felt the complete ballet music to be too long and the individual numbers too uneven in quality. Stravinsky also recognised the revisions of 1919 and 1945 as his criticism of his own composition.

According to Stravinsky, the models of Rimsky-Korsakov and Tchaikovsky are reflected in *The Firebird*, the former in its harmony and its treatment of the orchestra, the latter in a stylistic sense, e.g. in the 'Princesses with the golden apple movements (No. 7). By the abundance of novel instrumental effects (ponticello, col legno, flautando, glissando and flutter-tonguing) he nevertheless tried to outdo Rimsky-Korsakov. Stravinsky considered the music better than that of the other Russian ballets of that time, even if not very original. He was particularly proud of the instrumentation, which included a wealth of percussion and, in the stage band, Wagner tubas. The glissandos for horns, trombones and strings, which Rimsky-Korsakov had already employed before Stravinsky but were not yet known in the West, called forth the utmost astonishment from musicians and audiences. Stravinsky had taken over the means of differentiating between the human and the supernatural worlds in his music from Rimsky-

Korsakov's *Golden Cockerel*, completed in 1907 but first performed only in 1910 because of the censorship. The human world is associated with diatonic writing, the magical with Oriental sounding chromaticism or (particularly for Kashchei) pentatonicism. The constellation of the characters Kashchei, the Firebird and the prince is made clear musically also by the differentiation of the instrumentation at the appearance of the three protagonists. Stravinsky himself pointed out (in his *Memories and Commentaries*, 1960) that he had used two original Russian folk melodies: the *khorovod* theme of the 'Princesses' round dance' and the theme of the finale (both from Rimsky-Korsakov's *Hundred Russian National Songs* Op. 24 of 1876, nos. 79 and 21).

The first orchestral suite from *The Firebird* came into being in 1911 and was published by Jurgenson in 1912. For this the same plates were used as for the first edition of the complete score, and only the endings of the movements newly printed. The score of the second suite, for smaller orchestra, was dated February 1919 in Morges, and dedicated to the Orchestre de la Suisse Romande and Ernest Ansermet. Today the manuscript is located in the Bibliothèque Nationale in Paris (Rés Vma ms 8): the score was printed in 1920 by Chester in London. The composer's first piano reduction still included expression marks that he later omitted, as they no longer seemed appropriate to his new style (among others, *timidamente* and *sostenuto mystico*).

From the original 19 numbers Stravinsky chose five movements for the 1919 suite:

1. *Introduction. The Firebird and its dance. The Firebird's variation.* (No. 1, bars from Nos. 2 and 3, and No. 4 without the last 4½ bars of the original number)
2. *The princesses' round dance. Khorovod* (No. 10)
3. *Infernal dance of King Kashchei* (No. 16)
4. *Berceuse* (No. 17 with a new four-bar coda and six bars of the sostenuto *introduction* to No. 19)
5. Finale (No. 19 without the *introduction*)

The ballet suite of 1945 for the same orchestral forces first appeared from the Leeds Music Corporation. In this, the following movements are interpolated between the first and second movements of the 1919 suite (which show only slight modifications of the instrumentation as compared to the 1919 version):

a. *Pantomime I* (Bars 5–8 after figure 20 as well as figures 27 and 28 of the first edition)
b. *Pas de deux. The Firebird and Ivan* (No. 6 as far as figure 41)
c. *Pantomime II* (Figures 41, 53 and 54)
d. *Scherzo. Dance of the princesses* (No. 8)
e. *Pantomime III* (No. 9)

In *The Firebird* Stravinsky, through the combination of the Ballets Russes' balletic reforms and his virtuoso treatment of the orchestra, rhythmic complexity and already recognisable new expressiveness, pointed the way to his revolutionary works *Petrushka* and *The Rite of Spring*.

Herbert Schneider
Translation: Lionel Salter

VORWORT

Strawinskys Jugendwerke *Feuerwerk* und *Scherzo Fantastique* wurden zum ersten Mal am 6. Februar 1909 in einem von Alexander Ziloti geleiteten Konzert in St. Petersburg aufgeführt. Daran nahm auch Sergej Diaghilew teil, der von Strawinskvs Kompositionen beeindruckt war und der im weiteren Verlauf des Lebens von Strawinsky eine besondere Rolle spielen sollte. Da der Lehrer des jungen Komponisten, Nikolai Rimsky-Korsakow, am 8. Juni 1908 gestorben war, suchte Strawinskv einen neuen Förderer, der ihn dem Publikum präsentieren konnte. Diaghilew hatte seit 1906 seine Hauptaktivitäten nach Paris verlegt, wo er 1907 fünf Orchesterkonzerte und 1909 eine Saison mit fünf Balletten organisiert hatte. Zum Kreis Diaghilews gehörte der Tänzer und Choreograph Michail Fokin, der Maler Leon Bakst sowie der Tänzer Vaslav Nijinsky und die Primaballerina Tamara Karsavina. Seinen *Chroniques de ma vie* zufolge wünschte Strawinsky sich „dieser Gruppe fortschrittlicher und tatkräftiger Künstler anzuschließen, deren Seele Diaghilew war".

Die ersten Aufträge für Strawinsky waren die Instrumentierung des Nocturne As-Dur und des Valse brillante Es-Dur von Chopin für das Ballett *Les Sylphides* und die von Griegs *Kobold* für *Le Festin* (beide 1909), eine Tanzsuite nach Musik verschiedener Komponisten. Während die russischen Tänzer der Ballets Russes in Paris bereits Triumphe feierten, beendete Strawinsky in Ustilug den ersten Akt seiner Oper *Die Nachtigall*.

Die Kritik der französischen Presse an dem Mangel an russischem Kolorit oder russischer Atmosphäre, d. h. an Folklore-Elementen in den Ballets Russes war der Anlass für Diaghilews Wahl eines Stoffes, der das Russische stärker in den Vordergrund stellte. Er entschied sich für das Märchen vom Feuervogel, in das Elemente verschiedener anderer russischer Märchen integriert wurden.

Inhalt: Iwan Zarewitsch sieht eines Tages einen wunderbaren Feuervogel. Er verfolgt ihn, es gelingt ihm aber nur, ihm eine goldene Feder zu entreißen. Seine Verfolgungsjagd führt ihn in das Reich des bösen Kastchei, eines unsterblichen Halbgotts, der seiner habhaft werden und ihn wie zahlreiche andere Ritter und Prinzen in einen Stein verwandeln wollte. Die Töchter Kastcheis und die dreizehn gefangenen Prinzessinnen legen Fürbitte ein und bemühen sich, Iwan zu retten. Der Feuervogel erscheint und hebt den Zauber auf, indem er Iwan das Geheimnis von Kastcheis Unsterblichkeit verrät. Durch die Zerstörung des Eis, das sich in einem Kästchen befand, verliert Kastchei Leben und Zauberkraft. Das Schloss Kastcheis verschwindet, die Mädchen, die Prinzessinnen und Iwan bemächtigen sich der goldenen Äpfel seines Gartens.

Das Szenario, an dem auch Nijinsky, Bakst und Benois mitwirkten, entstand unter der Leitung von Fokin. Von Anatol Ljadow, der zunächst von Diaghilew mit der Komposition beauftragt war, verlangte er ein „russisches Ballett". Nachdem sich herausgestellt hatte, dass Nikolai Tscherepnins Entwürfe zu einer *Feuervogel*-Musik unbefriedigend waren und Ljadow kaum in der Lage gewesen wäre, die Komposition im vorgesehenen Zeitraum fertigzustellen, entschied sich Diaghilew für Strawinsky, der diese Chance zu nutzen verstand. Im Herbst 1909, nach der Rückkehr nach St. Petersburg, begann er mit der Komposition des *Feuervogel*, obgleich er noch nicht sicher sein konnte, den endgültigen Auftrag, für den schließlich ein Honorar von 1000 Rubel vereinbart wurde, für die Komposition des Balletts zu erhalten. Erst einen Monat nach Beginn der Komposition im Dezember kam Diaghilew nach Petersburg und war erstaunt, dass Strawinsky bereits mit der Arbeit angefangen hatte. Seit Anfang November hatte sich Strawinsky auf die Datscha der Familie Rimsky-Korsakow im Südosten von St. Petersburg zurückgezogen, kehrte im Dezember nach St. Petersburg zurück, wo er bis März die Komposition fertigstellte. Strawinsky spielte im Hause in der Straße Zamiatin Pereulok Diaghilew und seinem Kreis das neue Werk auf dem Klavier vor und wohnte, nachdem Fokin für jede fertige Szene bereits die Choreographie fertiggestellt hatte, auch den Proben der Ballets Russes bei. Die Orchesterpartitur und damit die Instrumentation vollendete Strawinsky einen Monat später. Das Ballettensemble reist im Frühjahr nach Paris. Mitte April wurde die Partitur nach Paris geschickt, wo Strawinsky im Mai während seines ersten Paris-Aufenthalts noch Details korrigierte und die Partitur am 18. Mai 1910 datierte. Das Autograph wird heute in der Bibliotheca Bodmeriana in Cologny (Genf) aufbewahrt und gehört dem Genfer Conservatoire.

Das opulente Bühnenbild und einen Teil der Kostüme hatte Alexander Golovin, die übrigen Kostüme (Feuervogel, Zarewitsch und Zarewna) Leon Bakst geschaffen. Unter der Leitung von Gabriel Pierné erlebte das Werk am 25. Juni 1910 in der Opéra in Paris seine sehr erfolgreiche Uraufführung. Tamara Karsawina (Feuervogel), Vera Fokina (Zarewna), Michail Fokin (Zarewitsch) und Alexis Bulgakow (Kastchei) waren die Hauptdarsteller. Während der Aufführungen lernte Strawinsky in der Loge Diaghilews zum ersten Mal die Pariser Berühmtheiten Proust, Giraudoux, Claudel, St. John Perse, Sarah Bernhardt und die Musiker Ravel und Debussy kennen, mit dem ihn bis zu dessen Tod ein freundschaftliches Verhältnis verband. Während der Erstaufführung ließ Diaghilew sogar Pferde auf die Bühne bringen, ein Effekt, der jedoch nicht wiederholt wurde. Fokin suchte die tänzerische Expressivität in der Umsetzung des Rhythmischen, nicht im Mimischen. Das Böse wurde durch groteske, eckige, hässliche und auch komische Bewegungen dargestellt. Die Ungeheuer hatten auf allen Vieren zu kriechen, zu hüpfen wie Frösche oder virtuos zu springen. Die Prinzessinnen tanzten barfuß, bewegten sich graziös und geschmeidig, während nur der Feuervogel durch eine Spitzentänzerin dargestellt wurde, die viele schwierige Sprünge auszuführen hatte. Nach Strawinskys späterem Urteil tanzten die Prinzessinnen geschmacklos süßlich, während die Tänzer das „non plus ultra" an roher Männlichkeit und Wildheit darstellten; in der Kastchei Szene haben die Tänzer auf dem Boden sitzend ihre Füße stupide hin- und hergestoßen. Die Choreographie von George Balanchine aus dem Jahre 1949/50 ist nach Strawinsky der von Fokin vorzuziehen, die von Chagall 1945 geschaffenen und bis 1970 in Aufführungen des New York City Ballet beibehaltenen Kostüme hielt der Komponist für die gelungensten überhaupt. Aus der Korrespondenz und den intimen Tagebüchern Gides, Claudels, Prousts u. a. wird deutlich, dass besonders die Diszipliniertheit und die Virtuosität der Solisten und die Betonung des männlichen Tanzes in den Ballets Russes die Zuschauer und die Intellektuellen gefangen nahm.

Entscheidend für den Erfolg des Balletts, dessen Handlung ziemlich schematisch und kaum dramatisch zu bezeichnen ist, war Strawinskys Musik, die Anna Pawlowa als zu kompliziert und zu bedeutungslos abgelehnt hatte. Die Musik des *Feuervogel* machte Strawinsky mit einem Schlag berühmt. Sie gehört bis heute zu den populärsten Stücken des 20. Jahrhunderts überhaupt. Als eines der wenigen Ballette blieb der *Feuervogel* auch im Repertoire der Ballets Russes. Der Komponist selbst war aber nicht mit der ursprünglichen Fassung zufrieden, die 1910 bei Jurgenson und später bei Schott erschien. Die ganze Ballettmusik empfand er als zu lang und die einzelnen Nummern als zu ungleich in ihrer Qualität. Als seine Kritik an der eigenen Komposition fasste Strawinsky auch die Bearbeitungen von 1919 und 1945 auf.

Die Vorbilder Rimsky-Korsakow und Tschaikowsky haben Strawinsky zufolge ihren Niederschlag im *Feuervogel* gefunden, Rimsky-Korsakow in der Harmonik und Orchesterbehandlung, Tschaikowsky in stilistischer Hinsicht, z. B. in dem Satz „Die Prinzessinnen mit den goldenen Äpfeln" (Nr. 7). Durch die Häufung neuer Instrumentationseffekte (ponticello, col legno, flautando, glissando und Flatterzunge) suchte er jedoch Rimsky-Korsakow zu übertreffen. Strawinsky hielt die Musik für besser als die der anderen Ballets Russes dieser Zeit, wenn auch nicht für sehr originell. Besonders stolz war er auf die Instrumentation, die ein reiches Schlagwerk und Wagnertuben in der Bühnenmusik einbezog. Die Horn-, Posaunen- und Streicherglissandi, die Rimsky-Korsakow bereits vor Strawinsky verwendet hatte, die aber noch nicht im Westen bekannt waren, riefen größtes Erstaunen unter den Musikern und Zuhörern hervor. Das Mittel zur Differenzierung der menschlichen und übernatürlichen Welt in seiner Musik hatte Strawinsky aus Rimsky-Korsakows 1907 vollendetem, aber wegen der Zensur erst 1910 aufgeführtem *Goldenen Hahn* übernommen. Die menschliche Welt ist mit der Diatonik, das Zauberhafte mit orientalisch wirkender Chromatik oder Pentatonik (besonders Kastchei) verbunden. Die Personenkonstellation Kastchei-Feuervogel-Prinz wird musikalisch auch durch die Differenzierung der Instrumentation beim Auftritt der drei Protagonisten verdeutlicht. Strawinsky selbst wies darauf hin (*Memories and Commentaries*, 1960), dass er zwei originale russische Volksmelodien verwendet hat: das Khorovod-Thema der „Ronde des princesses" und das Thema des Finale (beide aus Rimsky-Korsakows *Hundert russische Nationalgesänge* op. 24 von 1876, Nr. 79 und 21).

Die erste Orchestersuite aus dem *Feuervogel* entstand 1911 und wurde 1912 von Jurgenson verlegt. Hierfür wurden die gleichen Druckplatten wie für die erste Ausgabe der vollständigen Partitur verwendet und lediglich die Schlüsse der Sätze neu gefasst. Die Partitur der zweiten Suite mit reduzierter Orchesterbesetzung ist in Morges im Februar 1919 datiert und dem Orchestre de la Suisse romande und Ernest Ansermet gewidmet. Heute befindet sich das Manuskript in der Bibliothèque Nationale in Paris (Rés Vma ms 8), die Partitur wurde 1920 bei Chester in London gedruckt. Der erste Klavierauszug des Komponisten enthielt noch Ausdrucksbezeichnungen, die er später wegließ, da

sie seinem neuen Stil nicht mehr angemessen erschienen (u. a. *timidamente* und *sostenuto mystico*).

Aus den ursprünglich 19 Nummern hat Strawinsky für die Suite von 1919 fünf Sätze ausgewählt:

1. *Introduction. L'oiseau de feu et sa danse. Variation de l'oiseau de feu* (Nr. 1, Takte aus Nr. 2 und 3 sowie Nr. 4 ohne die letzten viereinhalb Takte der ursprünglichen Nummern)
2. *Ronde des princesses. Khorovode* (Nr. 10)
3. *Danse infernale du roi Kastchei* (Nr. 16)
4. *Berceuse* (Nr. 17 mit viertaktiger neuer Coda und sechs Takten der Sostenuto-*Introduction* zu Nr. 19)
5. *Finale* (Nr. 19 ohne *Introduction*)

Die Ballettsuite von 1945 für die gleiche Besetzung erschien zuerst bei der Leeds Music Corporation. Darin sind zwischen Satz 1 und 2 der Suite von 1919, die nur geringe Veränderungen der Instrumentierung gegenüber der Fassung von 1919 aufweisen, folgende Sätze eingeschoben:

a. *Pantomime I* (Takt 5–8 nach Ziffer 20 sowie die Ziffern 27 und 28 des Erstdrucks)
b. *Pas de deux. L'oiseau de feu et Ivan* (Nr. 6 bis Ziffer 41)
c. *Pantomime II* (Ziffer 53 und 54)
d. *Scherzo. Danse des princesses* (Nr. 8)
e. *Pantomime III* (Nr. 9)

Strawinsky wies im *Feuervogel* durch die Verbindung von Ballettreform der Ballets Russes mit seiner virtuosen Orchesterbehandlung, der rhythmischen Kompliziertheit und der bereits erkennbaren neuen Expressivität den Weg zu seinen revolutionären Werken *Petruschka* und *Sacre du printemps*.

Herbert Schneider

Autograph Score of the ballet
Page from 'Infernal Dance' (corresponding rehearsal number 109 of this score)

Autograph der Ballett-Partitur
Seite aus „Infernal Dance" (entsprechend Studierziffer 109 der vorliegenden Partitur)

L'OISEAU DE FEU
Ballet Suite 1945

1a. Introduction

Igor Stravinsky
(1882–1971)

No. 1389   EE 6772

6

1b. Prelude and Dance of the Firebird

8

1c. Variations (Firebird)

12

22

2. Pantomime I

3. Pas de deux
(Firebird and Ivan Tsarevich)

4. Pantomime II

5. Scherzo
(Dance of the Princesses)

6. Pantomime III

7. Rondo (Khorvod)

*) Starting as a separate number

8. Infernal Dance

82

9. Lullaby (Firebird)

120

10. Final Hymn

134